A Postcard from Sighet

The story of our family

Published in the UK by The Hoch Family

British Library Cataloguing in Publication Data

Hoch, Mordechai

A Postcard from Sighet

ISBN : 978-19133-1964-9

C 2020 Mordechai Hoch

Printed in Great Britain

CONTENTS

1. Introduction

Why, you may ask, would I write this story of our family now.

The events described here are most certainly exceptional, however they are not unique. Many Holocaust survivors have similar heroic stories, that if told, would astound. Stories of unbelievable suffering and incredible courage and these stories must never be forgotten.

In time, our memories fade. We must remember, try to comprehend and acknowledge what my parents, your grandparents and great grandparents endured in their young lifetime. Their battle for survival, their strength, perseverance and optimism for a better future must be told and not be forgotten, not just for their memory but for the benefit of future generations.

Their story is one of love, hope, courage and endurance in the face of adversity. I believe there are many lessons we can learn from it and adopt into our own lives, as its relevancy is timeless and everlasting.

This summary of our family story is dedicated to our children Arieh, Shira and Talia and our grandchildren Maya, Leila, Sam and Hannah; it is also for our future generations, in the hope that it will enhance their understanding of their place in the complex mosaic of our family history and that they can draw strength from its values into their own lives.

Mordechai Hoch

London, August 2020

2. Research

Most of the facts of our family history described here, I had to piece together over many years. Great Savta Rivka, my mother, your grandmother and great grandmother, was an Auschwitz survivor and as many other survivors, found it extremely difficult to talk about her experiences. Over the years, however, whilst Zvika and I were growing up, she divulged snippets of information. This created a sketchy picture of her experiences, enabling us to gain some understanding of her and her sisters' lives during WW2.

Both my parents, having experienced unbelievable hardship, misery and anguish, survived the Holocaust, though never underwent any therapy to deal with the aftermath of their terrible experiences during the war. My mother told me that they had made a pact, the horrors of the Holocaust should never be discussed at home especially not in front of the children, as they didn't want to bring a dark cloud into our home. The result of bottling up their mutual horrible experiences, had obvious long-term effects and consequences both to them and the childhood and adult lives of my brother and me.

In recent years, the understanding is that as well as Holocaust Syndrome, which was experienced by the survivors, the children of people who lived through the Holocaust are known as second-generation survivors. These children lived in the shadow of the Holocaust day in, day out and witnessed at first hand the affects its memories had on their parents. Their future was defined by their parents' experiences even though they had not lived through it.

It had been particularly difficult to learn of my Father's experiences during the war because he tragically died in 1956, I was only 7 and my brother Zvika was 4 years old.

I have always wanted to know more about my parents' lives before and during the war. The breakthrough came in October 1969, when I read an article published in the Israeli newspaper 'Maariv', describing the story of Hungarian slave labourers at the copper mines in a town called **BOR** in South-East Yugoslavia.

The article discussed the lives of Hungarian slave labourers in the Bor camp during 1943-4, including some horrific events that took place towards the end of war. Three thousand prisoners were led on a Death March by the Nazis, from the Bor mines in Yugoslavia towards Hungary. The article mentioned my father Lajosh (Arieh) Hoch by name. He was one of only three survivors of the massacre which took place on the 8th of October 1944, just before crossing the Hungarian border. A journalist, a Hungarian Jew named Kriel Gardosh, had written the article from first-hand experience as he was also one of the three survivors. I did meet him in his office in Tel Aviv, however he could not provide me with any further details.

The newspaper article provided Zvika and me with much information and opened an important window into our father's life which neither we, nor our mother were aware of. This increased our thirst to find out more about his story and in 1981, during a visit to Israel, Zvika and I decided to take a trip to Yad Vashem Holocaust memorial in order to access their archive for further information and to try and identify the third survivor.

We both travelled to Yad Vashem in Jerusalem and met the archivist dealing with the Yugoslavia chapter, Mr Zvi Zuker. He knew of the story of our father and showed us the huge archive in the basement, which was in complete disarray. He invited us to spend time and research it ourselves. Zvika and I immediately got to work and after three hours of sifting through endless documents, to our delight, we found the comprehensive firsthand testimony of the **'third survivor'**. Most details of the death march described here are based on his testimony.

A further link to the story was provided to us by a Serbian newspaper report we had found through the Jewish community in Subotica, Serbia, dated 14 January 1945. The article reported events concerning the death march and execution of 700 people in Crvenka, again, mentioning my father Lajosh (Arieh) Hoch by name as one of three survivors. It further stated that he gave evidence about the massacre from his hospital bed , where he was recovering from his injuries, to the local investigation committee.

My brother and I feel that this evidence, given by our father, is the last missing link to complete the story. Our aim now, is to obtain my father's original testimony from the authorities in Belgrade, as it describes his personal experiences in his own words. This we feel, will bring us closer to him and help us complete the puzzle.

3. The Family Tree

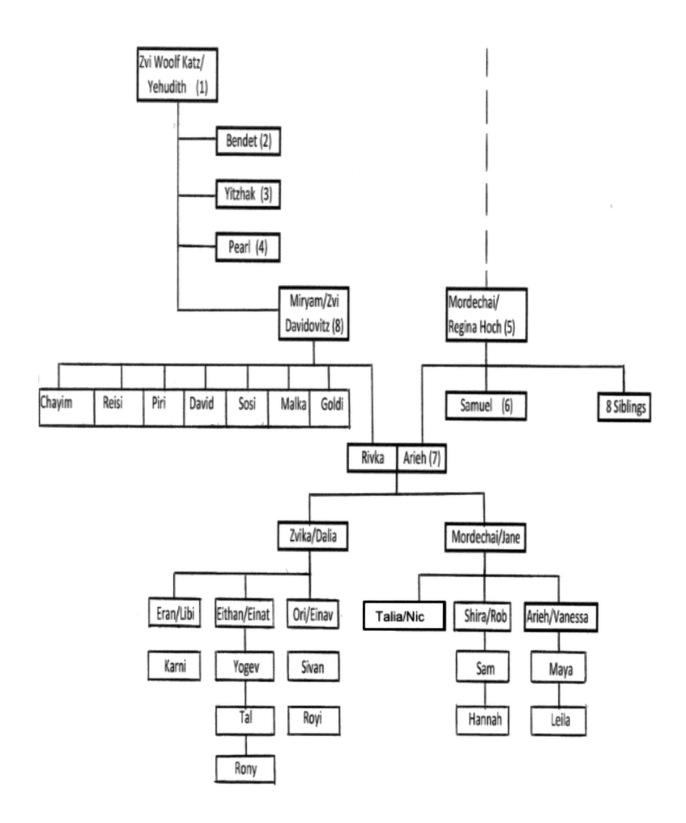

3.1 Narrative

1. Zvi Woolf (Hirsh)/ Yehudit Katz (maternal great grandparents)	Lived in Sighet. Yehudit was from Poland. Zvi was connected with the supply of meat. At special holidays like Passover, he would travel to Temeswar to buy goose fat, which was a delicacy.
2. Bendet (maternal great Uncle) (MIH)	Wife: Sarah **(MIH)*** Children: Yahad **(MIH)**, Malka **(MIH)**, Bluma **(MIH)**, Benjamin **(MIH)**, Hannah, Leah, Mordechai and Israel. Hannah, Leah & Mordechai emigrated to USA. Israel emigrated to Palestine
3. Yitzhak-Ber (maternal great Uncle)	Wife: Frida. Children: Yolanda. Yitzhak was blinded in WWI. They left Romania in 1937, immigrating first to Italy, then to Asmara in Ethiopia. Yolanda married a local ship Captain named Perli, they had three sons. They moved back to Italy at the end of WWII. They later moved to Caracas, Venezuela. We have met one of the sons Livio & wife Rebecca, who now live in the USA.
4. Pearl (maternal great Aunt)	Husband: Alter. Pearl was the younger sister of my Great Grandmother Miryam. She married at 18 and stayed with the older parents, as was custom with the youngest.
5. Mordechai Hoch/ Regina (my paternal grandparents)	My father's parents lived in Kabolapatak near Sighet, which was Hungary until 1920, it then became Romania. They had 7 sons and 2 daughters. We only have information about two siblings, Samuel and Arieh, my father.
6. Samuel (paternal Uncle)	Born: 15.10.1912, was a soldier on the Russian front. Died: 25.12.1942
7. Arieh Hoch /Rivka Davidovitz (my parents)	Children: Mordechai (me) and Zvika My father was the youngest sibling, born 20.8.1921. He died In Israel after a short Illness on 13.1.1956 aged 35.
8. Zvi Davidovitz/ Miryam Katz **(MIH)**, (my maternal grandparents)	Children: Goldi, Rivka (my mother), Malka, Sasha, Piri, Dudi, Reizi, Hayim **(MIH)**. Saba Zvi died in 1941, before the family were taken away. On arrival to Auschwitz Great Savta Miryam was taken to the gas chambers and murdered together with Hayim who was 12 years old. Goldi got married before the war and moved to Budapest, her husband was recruited to the Hungarian Army. When the Germans arrived in Sighet in March 1944, she came voluntarily back to Sighet to be with her sisters and was taken with them to Auschwitz. After the war she went back to Budapest, got married again and had one son Peter, who still lives there.

**MIH – MURDERED IN HOLOCAUST

4. The Holocaust in Sighet

With the entry of the Hungarian Army into Sighet on 5th September 1940, the conditions of the Jews worsened. The Hungarian governing bodies requested that each business carried a special license to trade, this made life very difficult for Jewish owned businesses.

The worst period for the Jews started in the summer of 1941. Thousands of Jews, who didn't have Hungarian citizenship, were displaced to other areas where they were murdered by the Hungarian army as well as the German Gestapo. Some were transferred to Ghettos and sent to Auschwitz.

On 19th February 1944 Ukrainian soldiers dressed in German uniforms appeared on the streets of Sighet.
Many of the men aged 20-48 were 'recruited' to work for the Hungarian army in the Slave Labour Brigades. Some were sent to the Eastern front and used to clear minefields for the army. My father's eldest brother Samuel was recruited to the Russian Army and sent to the Eastern front. In April 1944, arrangements were made to build two ghettos in Sighet. These were organised and planned and enabled the Germans and their co-perpetrators to round up 10-14,000 Jewish residents for the Final Solution. On 20th April 1944, overseen by the Hungarian gendarmes, all the town's Jews were moved into these ghettos.

Conditions in the Ghetto were dire with more than 10 people crowded into one room. The Sighet Jews were not allowed to possess valuables, they could not move around as they pleased and there was a lockdown and blackout between the hours of 17.00 to 06.00 in the morning. Treatment of the inhabitants was cruel, and they were used for various degrading work and manual labour. Sadly, this was just a preview of what was to come.

In the years leading to the war, life in the Davidovitz household was a happy one. My Grandparents were strictly religious and kept Shabbat and other Jewish holidays. They had eight happy and active children, two boys and six girls. My mother had told me that every Shabbat she used to walk by herself to the nearby village and visit her maternal grandmother Yehudit, with whom she had developed a special relationship with. She bought my mother gold earrings, which my mother said, made her feel very special and helped to differentiate her from her identical twin sister, Malka. That small house of Yehudit by the river, still stands to this day. My mother also told me that Elie Wiesel, the famous writer, was her neighbour and they used to play together as children.

In the few months the Jews were held in the Ghetto, they tried to make the best of it. They organised and maintained some kind of order in their lives. They created social help for the needy, employment exchange and even a police force to keep order. They continued their religious studying of Torah, created schools and developed some sort of framework for the children. The Sighet Jews believed that they would spend the rest of the war in the ghetto until the time they would be liberated. They were wrong, the first transport was organised and left for Auschwitz death camp on 16th May 1944.

The process was very painful and harrowing. Jewish people were gathered in the main synagogue, they were beaten and humiliated, especially the women and girls. They were then viciously loaded on cattle trains 70-80 people per carriage. The journey to Auschwitz lasted 3 days, they were without water, food or any sanitary facilities, except a bucket in the corner. The smell was overpowering and there were no windows or ventilation. Many people died on this terrible journey from dehydration, starvation or suffocation.

There were 4 transports of the Jews from Sighet and the surrounding villages, to Auschwitz, as follows:

- 16.5.1944 – 3,007 people
- 18.5.1944 – 3,148
- 20.5.1944 – 3,104
- 22.5.1944 – 3,490

In total 12,749 Jews were transported from Sighet.

5. Rivka: My Mother's story 1944 - 1945

In March 1944, the German army entered my mother's hometown, Sighet, they moved all Jews into the Ghettos and forced them to wear the yellow star. No one was allowed to go to work or leave the ghetto area. Their father Zvi had already died in 1941. Dudi, their brother, moved before the war at the age of 15 to live with his oldest sister Goldi in Budapest. When Goldi's husband was recruited to the Hungarian Army she decided out of a sense of responsibility as the oldest sister, to return to Sighet to be with her sisters, she left Dudi in Budapest.

In May 1944, all Sighet Jews were transported to Auschwitz. After their traumatic journey, the six sisters were separated from my grandmother and Chayim upon arrival. The sisters were young and strong and were declared fit for work. My grandmother and Chayim, who was 12 years old at the time, were sent 'elsewhere'.

It was later known that those detainees that were considered unfit to work including the elderly and young children were marched to gas chambers that were disguised as bath houses. Once inside, the prisoners were exposed to Zyklon-B poison gas. Chaim and my grandmother were sent to an extermination camp nearby and were dead within hours of arrival. My mother once told me that no one knew at the time exactly where they had been taken. She deeply regretted not being able to say her final goodbyes to her mother and brother and this regret haunted her for the rest of her years.

My mother and her sisters spent approximately 2 months in Auschwitz, working in the munition's factories in the area. Life was very tough; their living conditions were very crowded, and they were worked to exhaustion. They were given a watery soup and potato peelings once a day to eat, these provisions were not adequate, and they felt hungry all the time. Once, many years later, when my mother came to England to visit us, we went to TGI Fridays and when she saw potato skins on the menu, she couldn't stop laughing at the memory. She did try them for comparison, however eating them brought back sad memories for her.

In the camp they were woken up at 04.30 every morning and were forced to stand for hours in the freezing cold during the morning count. They wore only a thin dress and wooden clogs. The greatest difficulty for them was being able to see the smoking chimneys nearby in the adjacent extermination camp, there was a terrible smell which was always in the air. Shoshanna (Reisi), the youngest sister, who was only 15 and not very strong, was looked after by the sisters, they constantly told her to stand on her toes so she would look taller and they pinched her cheeks to make her look healthy.

It was well known that Dr Josef Mengele, a German physician who became known as the "Angel of Death", began working at Auschwitz from 1943. He performed a range of inhumane medical experiments on detainees and was in particular searching for identical twins for these experiments.

Out of the six sisters my mother and her sister Malka were identical twins. My mother told me that during the morning and evening count, five people were required to stand in each row. My mother and sister Malka ensured they never stood together in the same row, they always stood at a distance apart from each other so they could not be identified as identical twins by Mengele, who was constantly on the lookout for guinea pigs for his horrific medical experiments.

After 2 months of brutal life in Auschwitz, the sisters were transferred to a forced labour camp in **'Gelsenkirchen'**, Germany, they were again set to work in munitions factories. Once more, the conditions were very harsh, they had their heads shaved and they could hardly recognise each other. My mother told me during this time she was trusted by her German manager and acquired the reputation of being a good and responsible worker. Her manager put her in charge of the production team over the weekends as he preferred to spend the time with his family. On Monday morning, upon his return, he would whisper to her that he left something for her in the office, there she would find a piece of cake. This was such a treat and she always shared it with her sisters.

After approximately 5 weeks, the siblings were transferred yet again to another forced labour camp, this time in **'Sommerach'**, Germany. This was a very important munitions factory and because of this, was bombed by the Americans towards the end of the war. Many girls were killed however, my mother was saved by a large corrugated roof, which fell on her and covered her, thus saving her life. She told me that as she was lying there under the roof, she had a vision of her grandmother Yehudit, with whom she was very close, telling her not to be afraid and that she would survive this.

In January 1945, it was clear that Germany was losing the war. In order not to leave behind evidence of the slave labour operation, the factory workers were taken on a long and arduous march. Fifty-five German soldiers accompanied them, they walked for weeks, marching 30-40 kilometres each day. They had almost no water and given minimal food rations. At night, they slept in stables with nothing to keep them warm other than each other. Many of these prisoners fell on the road from exhaustion and various illnesses, they were killed or left to die.

Those prisoners that had survived the ordeal, eventually arrived starving and exhausted at a village called **'Groslippem'**. That evening they all slept in a cow shed however, the next morning no one came to wake them up, it was a very strange occurrence to wake naturally. They peered outside and saw the white flag of the Germans, who had surrendered as the Russian soldiers arrived that day. This was liberation day for them, the date was 15th May 1945.

My mother told me many times that the main reason they had survived the horrors they had experienced, was because the siblings were together and supported each other through the whole nightmare they endured. They gave each other the strength they needed to survive against all odds, millions of others were not as fortunate. After a few months of medical treatment, nourishment and recovery time, they all returned to their hometown, Sighet, to see who and what was left of their previous lives.

6. Arieh: My father's story 1944 – 1945

6.1 Background

The labour service system was a special feature in the history of the Holocaust in Hungary.

The Hungarian Prime Minister Horthy deemed certain members of society unreliable from a standpoint of National Security. The Hungarian regime was opposed to communists, members of ethnic minorities and especially Jews, who made up 8% of the population at the time. These groups were prohibited to serve in the Hungarian military service due to anti-Jewish laws, however, they didn't want to exempt these groups from sharing the burden of the national war effort, therefore, an Institution for unarmed military service, the 'Auxiliary Labour Service' was created.

Labour Service was forced labour, performed by labour battalions of mostly Jewish men, conscripted by the German Allied Hungarian regime. These units were stationed all over Hungary. Men were put to work in heavy construction and in my father's case, mine quarries. They were inadequately fed and poorly clothed and the gendarme and Army soldiers who guarded these slaves were vicious and cruel, often subjected them to violence, brutality and murder.

Whilst the labour service claimed many tens of thousands of Jewish lives, it is not considered as part of systematic genocide during the Holocaust. Some officers were determined and often succeeded in murdering Jews under their command, however, the Hungarian state did not originally set up the labour service system for elimination of conscripted Jewish males. The system as a whole cannot be defined as 'mobile execution grounds', even if in practice, they proved to be just that.

In an absurd twist, during the early stages of the German occupation, the labour service became a refuge for the doomed. Those that got conscripted for service escaped Auschwitz-Birkenau extermination camps. However, towards the last stages of the war, the majority of servicemen were delivered to the Germans who, in the winter of 1944-5, murdered countless numbers of Hungarian Jews under their command.

By the summer of 1943, an additional twenty labour companies were directed to support the German army. That summer the first labour companies also arrived in the copper mines of **Bor, Serbia**.

With the 6th April 1941 German invasion of Yugoslavia, the German army acquired large copper mines in the region of Bor, these were formerly French owned. This region in South-East Serbia, had valuable raw materials for the production of weaponry such as copper, nickel, tin and lead. From 1942 these mines provided 50% of Germany's total ore for its war efforts.

As the majority of Yugoslav Jews were annihilated already in 1942 and all Serbs were seen as potential partisans, the Germans turned to Budapest for the provision of 10,000 Hungarian workers for the works in Bor. On 2nd July 1943, the first German-Hungarian agreement was signed, this resulted in Hungary sending 3,000 recruits to Bor, in exchange for some of the raw materials mined there, followed by a further 3,000 following the invasion of Hungary by Germany on 19th March 1944. The majority of labourers were Jews (98%), amongst their ranks also included a small number of Sabbatarians about 18 (Christian converts to Judaism), members of minority churches (200), Romani people and Jehovah's witnesses (180).

The Labour force at Bor was housed in eight camps around the mines. The camps were under the control of the Hungarian army and work in the mines was supervised by armed members of the German paramilitary work organisation - the Organisation **Todt**.

While conditions varied slightly from camp to camp, treatment and accommodations for servicemen were acceptable on the whole until the end of 1943. However, when lieutenant Colonel Ede Maranyi took over as commander of the camps, beatings, truss-ups and executions became routine.

6.2 Life in Bor Labour Camp

Prisoners were transported to Bor in cattle cars. On one hand it appeared to them that their bad luck had caused them to leave the 'safe' camps at home for an unknown destination in Southern Yugoslavia. At the same time, they must have felt that at least they didn't have to go East towards the Russian borders, or worse, West to the German concentration camps. At this stage it was not generally known that these camps were in fact extermination camps. At the same time, in 1944, the final solution of the Hungarian Jews had commenced in earnest and there was an endless stream of loaded trains making their way towards Auschwitz.

At the railway station in Bor they were welcomed by a large group of German guards as well as a band of prisoners playing Mozart's Turkish March. Although this was somewhat comforting, the look of the prisoners did not instil much confidence, they looked like skeletons, shaven heads with a large Star of David painted front and back of their torn clothes. The groups were then housed along the railway line in pre-prepared camps at a distance of about 3 miles from each other.

Life in the camps was concentrated around four elements: hard labour, constant hunger, insufficient sleep and punishments. Guard duties and discipline were in the hands of the Hungarian soldiers, commanded by Captains, who were corrupt, deeply antisemitic and were generally uneducated.

Photo above shows the open copper mines at Bor.

The photo below shows slave labourers at the mine.

The photo above shows typical huts used as accommodation by the labourers.

On the first day, prisoners' shoes were replaced by wooden clogs, their head was shaven, and a Star of David was painted front and back on their shirts. The men were then divided into groups, equipped with tools and taken out to the fields to prepare a path for the laying of the railway to the next town. Although the Germans had supplied meagre food rations to the battalions, the Hungarian soldiers used the food to barter with the local villagers so the small amount that eventually got to the prisoners was barely enough to keep them alive.

In the evening, at the end of an 11-hour working day was the time for punishments. There was a 'blacklist' of the 'lazy' workers that was given to the Sergeant Major who, with German efficiency, used to punish them personally. The men were hung from their arms, toes barely touching the ground. Half an hour of this torture would normally be enough to break even the strongest. My mother told me that having a German name (Hoch), helped my father Arieh, the German's favoured him and allowed him to drive the locomotive train transporting the ore, this was an easier job.

Months passed uneventfully and in total isolation from the outside world. The only sign of the war being closer to an end was the huge number of American and British airplanes going overhead on their way to bomb the oil fields in Romania. The German and Hungarian soldiers began to seem increasingly worried. The punishments became rarer, this was the only sign that the prisoners had that the Germans were possibly losing the war and the end might not be away now.

The prisoners were not particularly surprised when one morning, at the end of August 1944, they were not taken out to work and were instructed to stay indoors until further notice. The Germans had given up the idea of clearing up the road and laying the railway, deciding instead to vacate the area.

The plight of the labour service of Bor was about to finish, the men could smell the end however there was still the question, what to do with the unwanted labourers? A few days passed and the men were told that they would begin a journey on foot to the Hungarian border. Around 3000 labourers were to leave first, the rest, a further 3000, would follow later. My father was selected to go with the first group.

6.3 The Death March and the massacre in Crvenka (pronounced Chervenka):

A historical overview

Following Romania's declaration of war against Germany on August 23rd, 1944 and the rapid advance of Soviet forces, the Hungarian army began evacuating the Bor camp complex.

On September 17th, 1944, the eve of Rosh Hashanah, the first group of approximately 3,200 prisoners began their 400-kilometre march towards Hungary. Supervised by 80–100 Hungarian soldiers, the men were given merely one loaf of bread and a tin of corned beef per person and told to make it last the whole journey. Men who were caught gathering food along the road or who had collapsed from exhaustion were beaten and even shot dead along the way.

Around September 27th, the group reached the German-occupied Western Banat (in northern Yugoslavia). Ethnic German militiamen dressed in paramilitary 'Deutsche Mannschaft' uniforms joined the Hungarian military personnel. They escorted the march all the way to the borders of the Hungarian-occupied Batschka. These militiamen reportedly jeered antisemitic slurs, beat the prisoners and shot any stragglers.

By October 6th an estimated 3,000 prisoners had reached the ethnic German-majority town of **Crvenka**, they had walked and survived the 400 kilometres from Bor. The labourers were locked into the premises of a brick factory operated by a company called Gläßer, Rauch & Welker. The prisoners in the brick factory in Crvenka would become both the victims and witnesses of a mass shooting during the night between October 7th and 8th .

Beginning at around 11 pm, the SS guards who had replaced the Hungarian soldiers (presumably members of the 31st SS Artillery Regiment of the 31st SS Grenadier-Division 'Böhmen und Mähren') ordered the prisoners to arrange themselves into rows of five. According to witnesses, the SS and even the Hungarian guards who had remained on the premises, forced the men to hand over any remaining valuables. The prisoners were marched away in groups of twenty to thirty, they were lined up near a large trench that had been emptied of clay for brick production. The prisoners were shot, methodically, group by group, until 700 or more had been murdered. Once the victims had toppled into the trench, the SS soldiers reportedly fired additional shots and threw hand grenades into the pit to ensure that every last man had died.

Map of the Death March

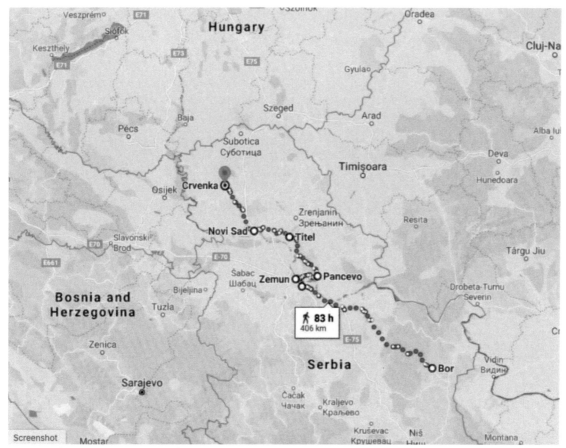

Route of the Death March from Bor to Crvenka, appx 400 Km.

6.4 The Death March – A Personal experience
(Based on the testimony of the Third survivor, found in Yad Vashem by Zvika & me)

"… On the 16 September 1944, 2 days before Rosh Hashanah, prisoners were told to be ready at midnight to leave on a march towards **Belgrade** and eventually towards the Hungarian border. We were given one loaf of bread (550 gram) and a tin of corned beef each and told this will be all the food available for the whole journey. A feeling of excitement spread amongst the prisoners, because they thought they were 'going home'.

The column of some 3,000 men, guarded by some 100 - 120 armed Hungarian soldiers, were on their way at midnight, a human column stretching along some 2 kilometres. Along the way, after walking some 10 hours, they collected a further 600 prisoners from another camp that joined them on their journey making the total of 3,600 prisoners.

On the evening of Rosh Hashanah some of the religious men prayed. All slept in an open field and it was very cold as they only had one thin blanket each - It was freezing. Early in the morning, the religious group had finished their prayers and even blew the shofar and then continued their way towards **Zagovitza.**

As we were walking in a populated area, hungry and thirsty, men tried to knock on doors asking for food or water. The Serbian population was very accommodating and stood outside their homes with food and water for the prisoners, but the guards had issued a command that anyone stepping away from the column would be shot. Quite a few men were shot along the way. Some of the prisoners stepped aside from the column to relieve themselves and were shot on the spot by the guards. Their friends had to dig their graves by hand to bury them.

Along the way the Serbian population tried to persuade the prisoners to escape and hide with them until the Russians arrived. Some did, but the majority preferred to stay in the 'safety' of the group in the belief that they are safer in larger numbers, rather than venture into the unknown.

We walked about 35-40 Kilometres every day, between large cities. As we approached a town, the guards surrounded us in order to stop us from asking for food or water. The order was to cross the town running. Try to imagine the run of so many people, stumbling over each other, most were bare footed, hungry and exhausted and whilst running, the guards were hitting the sluggers. Many fainted and were shot on the spot.

We slept in open fields, a distance of some 7-8 Kilometres from any town, with guards surrounding us, so that no one can escape. We used to walk daily up to 5 pm, but the sick that couldn't walk fast, dragged themselves along, arriving at the camp at 11-12 at night, only to have a brief rest and start again at 7 am the following day.

The distance to Belgrade is about 220 Kilometres and the main problem was shortage of water. People were prepared to give their last slice of bread or a cigarette for a drop of water. Up to **Belgrade**, we 'managed' somehow with food, which we prepared in advance before leaving Bor. However, we seemed a very sorry sight – dirty, tired, bleeding and infested with lice. Before entering Belgrade, we rested in a field during the day, a few Kilometres from Belgrade, since our guards wanted to prevent us from making any contact with the local population. However, as soon as we entered Belgrade, the Serb population came out of their houses flooding the streets in their thousands, in order to help the prisoners and disrupt the march. This caused great concerns to our guards, who started shooting at the Serbs, causing many casualties. During this mayhem we crossed the town through side roads and over the bridge towards the town of **Zeman**. We were locked in a large exhibition space for three days without any food or water.

The following day was Yom Kippur and some people started praying. Imagine the cries and the tears you could hear whilst prayers went on. I found that fasting the previous 4 days made it easier to fast another day.
In the evening we heard that we would continue our march the following day towards **Titel** and were each given some food; 200 gr bread, 20 gr margarine and 40 gr salami. Titel was about 95 Kilometres from Belgrade and the first town under Hungarian jurisdiction. During most of the way we walked in the rain, sleeping in open freezing fields without any cover. Most of the people have lost their shoes.

Whilst walking I overheard a conversation between a Hungarian guard and a German soldier; Asks the Hungarian "How many Jews did you shoot today?". Answers the German; "None". Replies the Hungarian; "What kind of German are you, don't you follow Hitler's orders?"

The Cruelty we experienced has reached new heights the longer the march progressed. We were given a few minutes rest every 15 Kilometres but were even not allowed to drink the dirty water by the roadside . We progressed towards **Oyvidek** and then to **Sombor** and onwards to **Santomash**.

Throughout, the Serbian people were very hospitable and felt sorry for us, although couldn't do much in the presence of the guards. In contrast, the German population in the area (called Schwabs), displayed animosity and weren't prepared to help at all. On the contrary, they drew the guards' attention to anyone leaving the column.

As we progressed, we saw evidence of the Germans' retreat. Military vehicles, soldiers and German civilians were all heading north towards the Hungarian border. Finally, we arrived at the town of **Crevenka** and housed in a brick-making factory. We were told to stay put and noticed that the Hungarian guards are collecting their belongings and leaving. We had a bad feeling and asked some young guards what's happening, but no one would answer. People were afraid and tried to leave, but the place had been well guarded. At 10 pm, the German SS soldiers arrived. Our hearts sank as we were prepared for the worst, but on the other hand found it hard to believe they will kill so many people, when the Russians are only some 20 Kilometres away.

The following day, the SS started shooting in the air as if they were playing and it lasted the whole day. Later, we realised they were preparing the neighbouring population, so that when the killing starts, the shooting would appear as 'normal'.

The SS instructed that we stand in rows of 10 and we stood still from 3pm-9pm without moving or talking. We haven't eaten for 5 days and were totally exhausted and terrified of what is coming. We were left alone until 10.30 pm, A group of SS men came in and asked us to hand over all our valuables, saying we won't need them anymore. People handed over the very few valuables they still possessed, as watches and money.

Then, they started taking the men in groups of 20 towards the large ditch in the adjacent courtyard. We heard the shots mixed with cries and then silence. They came to take another group and another group, every 3 minutes. My turn came with the 10th group of 20 men, led by 6 SS soldiers. The size of the ditch was 50 metres long by 10 metres wide by 1.5 metres deep. The order was as follows; 4 SS on each side guarding, with 2 SS on the other sides responsible for the shooting. Each group of 20 were led alternately to the right or the left side. They were shooting from a distance of 3 meters. My turn came, I was shot and fell bleeding profusely into the ditch. The bullet hit my neck, entered under my ear and came out clean by the side of my nose. I lay there motionless for a couple of minutes. When they threw more bodies on top of me, I pretended to be dead and took cover under the bodies in order not to be hit by any straying bullets. From time to time the SS shone torches into the ditch, looking to ensure no one is alive. For good measure they also threw grenades into the mass of bodies.

It's hard to describe what I thought and felt during those hours of lying badly wounded, bleeding and covered by so many bodies. The constant shooting through the night has deafened me and with the bodies falling all over my head, a lot of blood kept pouring all over me. Despite my pains, I fell asleep for a short time.

I had been shot at around midnight and the shooting continued until about 5 am. The morning came and I noticed the deep silence. No one was around as all the SS soldiers disappeared. I managed to climb somehow out of the ditch, covered in blood and mud and feeling very thirsty. I suddenly saw two more prisoners climbing out of the ditch and we headed away towards the nearby corn field, hoping to find some shelter, food and medical attention to our wounds. The names of the other two survivors were Kriel Gardosh (the Israeli Journalist who wrote the original story) and Lajosh (Arieh) Hoch, who was wounded in the left arm from a grenade shrapnel that was thrown into the ditch, to ensure they were all dead.

(My father was not shot in the head like the other men, probably because he jumped into the ditch just before being shot, pretending to have been shot and thus survived with a relatively light wound above the elbow, that paralysed his left arm).

As we covered some ground, we heard the voices of a number of SS who were chasing us and firing their weapons at us for about 2 Kilometres. The three of us hid in a nearby corn field about 6-7 Kilometres from Crvenka and rested there for the night.

My father told the story that when the morning came and the local farmer walking his dog had spotted the three hiding, he approached and whispered, "I have noticed you, don't be afraid, keep still and quiet and I will return in the evening to collect you".

Indeed, when darkness fell he returned and endangering his own life, he took us to his farmhouse and provided us with a meal we have not seen in many months of hot milk, fresh bread, butter, eggs and housed us in the nearby stable, where we stayed for a couple of weeks. During the day, numerous Serb families came to visit the three of us in the stable, bringing with them food, cooked meals and even grapes and wine. As German SS were still patrolling the streets, the Serb host family were taking a very great risk to their lives in protecting the three Jewish men.

We spent our time eating, resting and waiting for the Russians to arrive. When the Russians finally arrived, the Serbs in the village embraced us and offered us their houses to rest and recuperate. The Russians, upon hearing our story were angry and swore to take revenge on our behalf.

In time we learned the fate that met the Jewish people in the various extermination camps, especially Auschwitz. The Serbs felt so sorry for us that have welcomed us to stay in the village and even promised to find us suitable wives, since where else can we go after this holocaust? And who knows if anyone from our families has survived?

We stayed there a further 3 weeks, when we heard that many survivors are making their way to Romania, where the 'Joint' organisation had established camps to assist the returning refugees. We made our way to **Temeswar**, where we were given clothes and food stamps. This is where the three of us parted company, as the other two decided to make their way back home to **Sighet**..."

7. After the war - Sighet

The town of Sighet was liberated by the Red Army in October 1944. The first Jews returning were young men that served in the various labour camps throughout Europe. The meetings amongst the Holocaust survivors were very emotional, mixed with many tears and laughter. My father returned in early 1945. Unfortunately, he was the only member of his large family that survived (he was the youngest of 9 children). Many did not return. Many survivors, who witnessed the horrors of the Holocaust decided to leave for Palestine or to other countries, mainly the US.

In the meantime, in an attempt to rebuild the community and restore Jewish life in Sighet, the returnees established soup kitchens, a hospital, a school, libraries and a synagogue. In 1947 there were more than 2,000 Jews living in Sighet.

My uncle David, my mother's brother, who was nicknamed Dudi, (now living in Haifa), had returned in early November 1944 to Sighet, it looked like a ghost town. His first action was to put up a memorial headstone to their father Zvi, who died in Sighet in 1941, because when he died, they didn't have the means to put it up.

Dudi found that their old house was completely destroyed by a bomb. He was invited by his neighbours the Stern family to take over their large house, since they had decided to leave immediately for Palestine. Dudi got the place ready and waited for the return of his sisters and when they did, they all moved into the Stern's house.

Everyone was looking for work. My father, who had before the war helped his uncle manage his brush manufacturing factory, decided to open an off license and owned it for about a year.

The oldest sister Goldi, having come through the horrors of the Holocaust, decided to move back to Budapest, there she re-married and had one son called Peter. He now lives in Budapest, I met up with him there in the year 1999. He previously came to stay with us in the UK for Arieh's Bar Mitzva in 1986.

My mother and father, who vaguely knew of each other through a youth movement, before the war, got together again and married in 1946.

Notice in the photo below how happy and handsome they both looked on their wedding day, it is hard to believe that they went through so much in the last few years and only a few months before, came out of hell.

All my mother's sisters got married before embarking on the journey to Palestine.

The wedding day of my mother (Rivka) and father (Arieh) in Sighet in 1946.

8. Destination Palestine

In early 1947, my mother, father, my aunt Malka (Savta's twin sister) and her husband Shmuel (Fifi), decided to travel to Palestine and began their journey. Their first destination was Budapest, but unfortunately they were stopped on the way by Hungarian border police. During the argument that ensued, they managed to escape by bribing a van driver that was parked nearby, to take them to Budapest.

They arrived in Budapest on Saturday and headed straight to the Rabbi's house. From there they continued through Austria and then through Italy. Along the way, they met many refugees heading in the same direction. They were invited by the Jewish organisation called 'Habricha' (Translated from Hebrew 'The Escape'), to stay in a large house belonging to a wealthy Italian Jew called Vitali, together with some 60 other refugees.

Villa Vitali was in a small village called Val Madonna, in the region of Alessandria, near Milan. They stayed there for a few weeks then they made their way South towards the town of Bari in Southern Italy, on the Adriatic shores. Here they waited patiently to board the ship that would eventually take them home, to the promised land, Palestine.

In the photo below you can see my mother Rivka(on the right) and her twin sister Malka, together with their husbands, my father Arieh (right) and Uncle Shmuel, exploring nature and relaxing in the hills around Bari Italy, whilst waiting for a boat to take them to Palestine.

My father was very dapper, notice the tie and his fancy shoes? (Maybe this is where our son Arieh gets it from). The photo was taken in 1947, they were 26 years old here and looked very relaxed, happy and safe, looking forward with great anticipation to their journey to their final destination, Palestine.

9. Aliya Bet

Aliya Bet or in simpler terms, illegal immigration to Palestine during the British Mandate, was organised by the Mossad. It was an arm of the Hagenah underground organisation in Palestine, an organisation established before the creation of the State of Israel in May 1948. Aliya Bet was sustained by the Zionist dream, spurred by the threat and later by the unrelenting actuality of Nazi annihilation. One hundred and twenty-five thousand Jewish men, women and children made the perilous journey by sea to Palestine during the period 1938-1948, despite the many obstacles placed in their way by the adamant opposition, the British government.

Many Jews, desperate to reach Palestine, voluntarily submitted to travelling in dangerous, old and filthy ships that were hopelessly overcrowded. Clandestine landings at night on secluded stretches of beach in Palestine often went wrong and some ships wandered the Mediterranean, their unfortunate passengers stranded for weeks on end.

In America, many young men who were veterans got recruited. Ships were purchased surreptitiously for use in this operation. Ten ships came from America, manned by American volunteers, the most famous of which was Exodus. Shiploads of Holocaust survivors arrived in Palestine under the guns of the Royal Navy, the image of Britain's proud warships fighting impoverished Holocaust survivors eventually broke down British resistance, this led Britain to give up its Palestine mandate in 1948. On 15 May 1948 the creation of the State of Israel was announced.

10. The Voyage

At midnight on the 13 May 1947, with the aid of rubber dinghies, they boarded the ship 'Mordei Hagetaot' (translated 'The Ghetto Fighters'), at the port of Metaponto near Bari, Italy, commanded by Eliezer Armon, together with a further 1,457 refugees – 902 men, 518 women and 37 children. The ship was to rendezvous at sea with a ship called 'Yehuda Halevi' and take on board its 399 refugees. This rendezvous never took place because 'Yehuda Halevi' had pulled into the port of Palermo, Sicily, to fuel and to care for a sick girl on board.

Above: The 'ship' Mordei Hagetaot (The Ghetto Fighters), in which my parents shared the journey with 1,457 immigrants, making their way to Palestine.

An immigrant ship moored at Haifa, confronting British soldiers. The caption reads: "THE GERMANS DESTROYED OUR FAMILIES, DON'T YOU DESTROY OUR HOPES".

The sailing was very rough, on the 15th May a terrible storm blew, the ship needed to take shelter for 34 hours before being able to resume its journey. On 23rd May, as they approached the shores of Palestine near the Arab town of Rafiach, which was opposite Gaza, 'Mordei Hagetaot' was spotted by a British reconnaissance plane. Several hours later, the ship was surrounded by two British destroyers, who rammed the vessel and prevented the ship from approaching the port. The British soldiers mounted the ship using tear gas and water cannons, a fight broke out between them and the refugees, they were determined not to be taken off the ship and gave as good as they got. The stand-off and ensuing battle lasted for about 3 hours. The ship was eventually towed to the Port of Haifa and the refugees were transferred to a British ship 'Runny-mead Park', they were transported the following day to a refugee camp in Cyprus. The Captain, Armon continued with the refugees to Cyprus however the other members of his crew hid in a pre-prepared hideout on the boat. They were freed the following day by a crew of port workers that had come to clean the vessel.

The British government had created the camps in Cyprus as part of its effort to stem the rising tide of 'illegal' immigration to Palestine which was organised by the Zionist movement's Ha'apala or Aliya Bet (illegal immigration) campaign.

Nearly all the detainees were Holocaust survivors. Many had fled from Eastern Europe or the Soviet Union, with the help of the underground 'Ha'Bricha' movement. The Cyprus detainees sailed on 39 ships from ports in France, Italy and the Balkans.

In all, the British detained about 52,000 refugees in Cyprus, including about 1,300 from North Africa. The Cyprus detainees were primarily young people who had joined Zionist youth groups before departing Europe. Approximately 80% were aged 12-35. The majority were orphans.

The British military ran the detention camps in accordance with the harsh model of the Prisoners of War camp (POW). All the British camps in Cyprus were well fenced with barbed wire and watch towers and were well guarded. Living accommodation was basic, in tents and tin huts that became unbearably hot in the summer and freezing cold in the damp, rainy winter. They had little furniture, no electric lighting, limited access to water, bad food and poor sanitary conditions.

My father and mother stayed in the Cyprus camp for about a year, waiting for permission to enter Palestine. The Joint Distribution Committee (JDC) provided for the welfare of the detainees, including supplying food and medical care. They were given basic food which they cooked themselves, but because they ate only Kosher food, they received Kosher meat only on Friday for Shabbat.

The camp in Cyprus. Living accommodation was in tents or tin huts.

In May 1948, upon the establishment of the State of Israel, my parents were finally given permission to enter Palestine and they settled near Hadera. Three months later on 15th August 1948, I was born.

We found accommodation in Haifa , moving two years later to a small village called Zarnuga near Rehovot, it was here that Zvika and I spent our childhood.

11. Letters from the Journey

In 2005, I met for the first time my second cousin Livio. Livio was the son of Yolanda Perli, who was my mother's first cousin and best friend. Our meeting was very emotional, especially as Livio was unaware of his vast family in the UK and Israel. During one of our conversations, Livio mentioned that he had letters that my mother wrote to Yolanda from the camp in Cyprus. I recall that in the late 1950's Yolanda came to visit my mother in Israel.

These letters were a real find. I translated them and have included them below as I feel they serve as important first-hand documents, they provide a window into my parents lives at that time and help us understand the frame of mind of our close relatives, who had survived the Holocaust and then shortly after finding themselves interned in another camp in Cyprus.

The following is the first letter written to Yolanda and her family, from their temporary accommodation Villa Vitali in Valmadona, Italy.
Yolanda and her family left Sighet in 1937, well before the start of World War II.

31/12/1946
Valmadona, Italy

My Dears

We have received the letter, which brought us great happiness, and now that we have an exact address, we are writing with joy, hoping that you will receive our letter.

We cannot write much about ourselves, especially about the experiences of the concentration camps. As we gather, dear uncle does not know about anything. We are pleased that at least some of the family did not have to go through what we have gone through. If they would have told us what we will be subjected to, we would rather have committed suicide; I would have done that anyway.

On the 15 May 1944, we had been deported, along with our dear mother, to the famous Auschwitz camp. Upon arrival, we have been separated and have not met since. After spending 8 weeks there, we have been transported to Germany to a forced labour camp, where we have worked for one year in difficult conditions, exposed to starvation and witnessing the Germans' passion for executions.

We were liberated on the 9th May 1945, and were eager to return to our birthplace, Sighet, hoping that we will find someone there. Unfortunately, we have not found anyone, apart from our brother David. Giving thanks to G-d that we have at least met. We have tried to forget the past, but is it at all possible to forget?

After arriving in Sighet we got married and since there was no purpose in staying there, as all the other Jews, we have decided to hurry out of Europe. Some made their way to America or Brazil, but we have chosen Palestine. We knew only too well that initially there would be difficulties, as our financial situation is not the best, considering that our journey so far had cost us a great deal.

Our husbands are both from Marmaros Sighet and are both very decent, well-meaning men. We would like you to send us a photo of the whole family, as we are very curious about you. We will also send some photos next time.

If possible, please reply immediately with photos and we conclude this letter with great love and kisses to you all.

Rivka, Malka and our husbands

****
9/1/1947
Valmadona, Italy

My Dears (to Yolanda)

We received your letter which we read with great joy and we rush to reply, in the hope that you will exchange our letter with another one soon.
Thanks to G-d we are well, in good health and grateful to the good G-d that we evaded that hell and not suffered some illness, as unfortunately a great many people did.

We are in a villa with sixty others, who have been waiting for three months to leave for Palestine. Other than us, there are many others here in Italy who wish to go. We hope that we will leave soon.

We promise that wherever in the world we will be, we will always write to you, because we can feel your joy in receiving letters from us – we, who have returned from the other world. But unfortunately, our dear mother, along with our twelve-year old little brother, stayed behind. Our dear father had the fortune to die at home in 1941. Initially, we were sorry of course, but later in hindsight, we were glad he didn't die in the camp.

We have written enough about ourselves and feel our experiences cannot be described in such simple terms, as even we cannot believe that we have lived through such monstrosity.

Write about yourself a lot, how is the dear Aunt, Uncle and you, Jolanka, with your family? Write where you have been during the war, we hope you didn't suffer? I end this letter and will write more next time. Kisses to the dear Aunt, Uncle and Jolanka with her family.

Malka, Rivka; Our husbands are also sending their regards

****

4/6/1947
From Cyprus camp

Dear Uncle Zeigler (Yolanda's father Itzik Ber)

We have been in Cyprus for a week now. Thank G-d we are fine – that we can say. We cannot write much, as we are not free. The journey was very difficult and dangerous, and we have been returned from Haifa. It is difficult for us, but we are forced to turn to the Uncle for a little help, despite the fact that we don't know how you are financially.

We are asking the Uncle and also you Jolanka, to please help us with a food parcel, some tobacco, or a few dollars or a few Palestine pounds. When the good G-d will help us and we reach Palestine, we will repay all of it. Dear Jolanka, please write home that we are here, because we cannot write much.

We send kisses to you, with great family love
Rivka, Malka and our husbands

****

8/6/1947
From Cyprus camp

Dear Uncle Zeigler

Perhaps the Uncle will be surprised to hear that we are in Cyprus, instead of Palestine. But all Jews who are on this journey must go through this. We are with 15,000 Jews who are awaiting their turn, and each month a certain number of people are transported legally to Palestine.

Otherwise, we are well; If you could, please help us by sending a food parcel, or a few dollars or Palestine pounds and when the good G-d will help, we will return it.

I am not going to write more, as I cannot write a lot and end this letter with a lot of family love, together with our husbands who also send their regards.

Rivka and Malka

12.   The Promised Land

12.1   The first 8 years: 1948-1956

When my parents first arrived in Palestine on 17th July 1947, they stayed at the Brandes Village. My mother was in her 7th month of pregnancy with me. Initially they lived in temporary accommodation in what was a tented village, outside Hadera. Here the living conditions were not the most salubrious, to say the least. One month later, my mother travelled to a hospital in Hadera and gave birth to me on 15th August 1948.

We moved to a small two bedroom flat in Bat Galim, downtown Haifa, the house had been abandoned by Arabs. The street was called Madregot Teiman (Yemen steps). We lived there for about two years, together with two of my mother's sisters (Sosi and Piri) and their husbands .

Photo above: My mother and me as a baby, Haifa, 1948.

Although I was only two years old at the time, I remember the flat, the stairs, some of the décor and a nice old lady called Auntie Pearl, who used to feed me boiled sweets, I still remember the box.

Finding work in those days had been a major challenge. My Dad, as many other new Olim, tried his hand at various jobs, at some point he even became a fisherman. Together with Uncle Dudi, they formed a company and supplied fish to restaurants and various clients. For a while they were doing quite well, so much so, they came to the attention of a large national cooperative in Haifa 'Tenuva'. Their success became a problem for Tenuva, who decided to undercut them by reducing prices to a minimum, in order to knock them out of business, which of course, they succeeded in doing.

My father decided to venture out and travel South, searching for other opportunities, mainly in the building trade. In his search, he arrived at a small Arab village outside the town of Rehovot called

Zarnooga, there he found an abandoned small house with an adjacent small plot of land, which was where we settled.

I can remember my Dad building a small holding, bringing in a few cows, chicken, geese and ducks. I also remember him planting six fruit trees in our front yard, we had apples, pears, plums and a guava tree bearing red fruit. My job was to water the trees once a week. Without much background, preparations or training, we became small 'farmers'. It was a huge culture change, especially for my mother Rivka.

As the building trade was buoyant at that time my Dad had started his own company with five other partners, making foundations and drilling piles for new buildings. They had no mechanical machinery, so all the work had to be done manually. This was very hard physical work however my father was young and strong, he battled on despite his war injury which limited his movements in the left hand and the company became quite successful.

I remember during my school holidays, my Dad took me on site with him, he was so proud to show me his official stamp as MD of the company, which he stored in an attractive small silver box.

We were not well off by any means, we had no electricity and had to rely on paraffin lamps until 1960. There was no running hot water and we only had an outside toilet. Though I do remember being a happy child, doing well in school and knowing that I was loved, especially by my father, who doted on me. I loved it when he came home at the end of a hard day's work and we would sit together on the stone path leading to our house to have a 'chat.' He used to let me drink the leftovers of his sweet cold tea from the thermos, which tasted great. I suspect he deliberately left some tea in the thermos for me for our little 'chats.'

The first few years of my childhood, growing up with Zvika, were happy. I had many friends and used to spend endless hours outdoors, playing together and getting into all sorts of mischief. Some of those friends are still around today, especially a good friend called Arieh Shtauber. We are still in touch and always meet whenever I am visiting Israel.

12.2   1956

My father, Great Saba Arieh, died on 13th January 1956 after a short illness. I was only seven years old however I remember so vividly everything that happened around that time; visiting him at the hospital, our last goodbye, his funeral and having to get up every morning, come rain or shine at 5.30, in order to go to synagogue and say Kaddish for a whole year. I can distinctly say that this was the moment my childhood, at the age of seven, came to an end and I became the 'man of the house'. Without any means of support, my mother Rivka had to search for a job. She found one as a seamstress in the nearby town of Rehovot, a 45-minute bus ride from home.

Zvika was only three and half when my father died, and my mother had to go out to work. She was out daily between the hours of 7am-8pm. At the age of seven, I became my brother's carer. I prepared him for nursery and then school. I made us breakfast and dinner, poor Zvika had to have scrambled eggs, olives with bread and butter every evening, that was all I could prepare. Every evening I put him to bed.

Zvika was a high-spirited child and many times ran away from school. Children would come and tell me when he had escaped (again) and I would leave my class with permission, to chase him around the fields and bring him back. I realise now that he was going through a tough time and this behaviour of his was a cry for attention.

We had no babysitters, they were non-existent at the time, therefore I had to take this on whilst continuing my studies, homework, I had very little spare time for play. I didn't mind the responsibility, as I knew that I was helping our mother with everything I do, after all, I was 'the man of the house'. However, this was a heavy responsibility for any seven year old and a steep learning process during which our childhood had been put on hold and we had to mature almost overnight.

My brother Zvika and me, 1957

12.3   1960 and Beyond

My mother Rivka was the most amazing and resourceful woman, especially when it came to saving money. After 4 years of working, she was able to buy a flat in Rehovot into which the three of us moved in 1960. She always wanted a better future for Zvika and I, she made enormous personal and financial sacrifices to achieve this.

I remember my mother telling me much later in life, that when my father Arieh was ill in hospital and realised his condition was critical, he made her promise him that she would always ensure that their children would study. She was always so proud that she was able to fulfil this promise to him.

I will always be indebted to her and eternally grateful for all she did for us, the love and care she gave us, but especially, the gift of our education. With very little means and despite difficult circumstances, she was determined to keep her promise to our father and ensure that both Zvika and I had the best education possible. A great source of pride for her was that she was able to see us both qualify from the Haifa Technion in the 1970's. I was so happy she was able to enjoy it after all her hard work and many sacrifices.

In summary, as I said initially, this is a story of love, courage and endurance. I hope that through reading this 'brief' history of our family, you will understand your ancestors better as 'real' people and be able to take away some positive attributes that may inspire and help you at some point in your own lives in future.

So, my dear children, our story continues on with your generation, with you, your children and all the future generations of our wonderful family. This is not the end, but simply "to be continued" …

12.4   Gallery of photos.

Above: The Davidovitz siblings in 1968 in Israel, from left, My mother Rivka,Reisi (Shoshana), Piri (Penina), Dudi (David), Sosi (Sasha), Malka (Rivka's twin) and Goldi the eldest sister. They have all been through and experienced the terrible Shoah but survived, endured and flourished because of the strong bond, care and love they had for one another.

My mother: Rivka Hoch nee Davidovitz
1921-2017

My father: Arieh Hoch
1921-1956